10/2015

To Nina, Ellie & Anna -
Don't forget to hug your
MONSTER everyday!! :)

Laura Grimball

MOMSTER

Written by Laura Jensen-Kimball

Illustrated by Peter Mahr

MOMSTER

© 2014 by Laura Jensen-Kimball. All rights reserved. No portion of this book may be reproduced in any form without the written permission of Laura Jensen-Kimball.

Written by Laura Jensen-Kimball
Illustrated by Peter Mahr

Printed by Christian Printers, Inc. 1411 21st St., Des Moines, IA, 50311

ISBN 978-0-9963646-0-7 (8.5x11 Edition)
Library of Congress Control Number: 2015909123

Printed in the United States of America

Visit Wackystackbooks.com for more information on MOMSTER

This book is dedicated to my four children, Dean, Grant, Brooke and Jack, who have transformed me into a **MOMSTER** and back many, many times. I love you guys.

Listen to me children, I have crucial news to tell!
Every kid should know this, it will surely serve you well!
I know the truth about our moms and you should all beware-
Our mothers aren't what you think, please listen if you dare!

I was minding my own business, simply watching the TV-

When my mother nicely asked,
"Honey, will you please come help me?"

It didn't sound important, so I finished the cartoon-
Mom called a few more times and then she barked like a baboon!
I figured I'd go help her when my silly show had ended-
So I yelled out, "In a sec!" I hope she's not offended.

The bark became a shout, then a frightening, mighty roar!
I heard stampeding, stomping feet, and pounding on the floor.
Next I heard the snarling, the growling and even grunting too-
What is happening to my mom? She sounded like a zoo!

The noise was getting louder so I thought I'd better see–
That is when I saw it...a MOMSTER, and she was coming after me!

A MOMSTER, a MOMSTER, her face as red as a lobster!
Her spit was flying to the floor, her eyeballs popping out-
Her hands were curled up with claws and -WOW- could that thing shout!

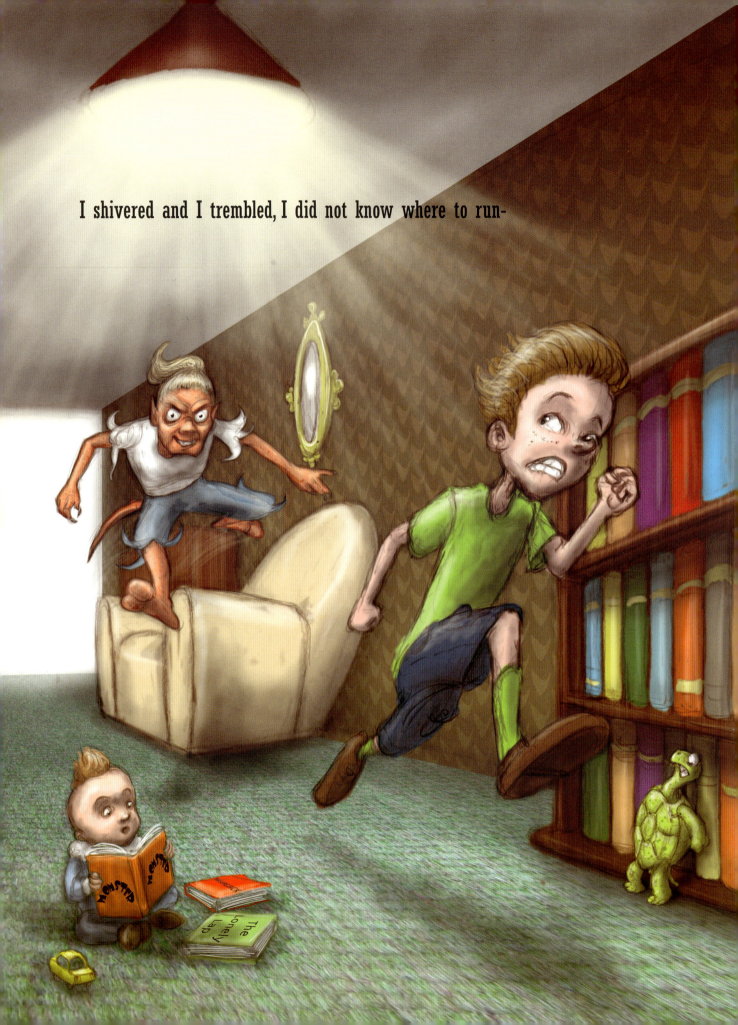
I shivered and I trembled, I did not know where to run-

Quivering with fear, I didn't know what to say-
So, I sweetly asked my MOMSTER, "Um, d-did you have a good d-day?"
She continued to draw towards me, no smile or luck in sight.
I have got to warn you that MOMSTERS are a fright!

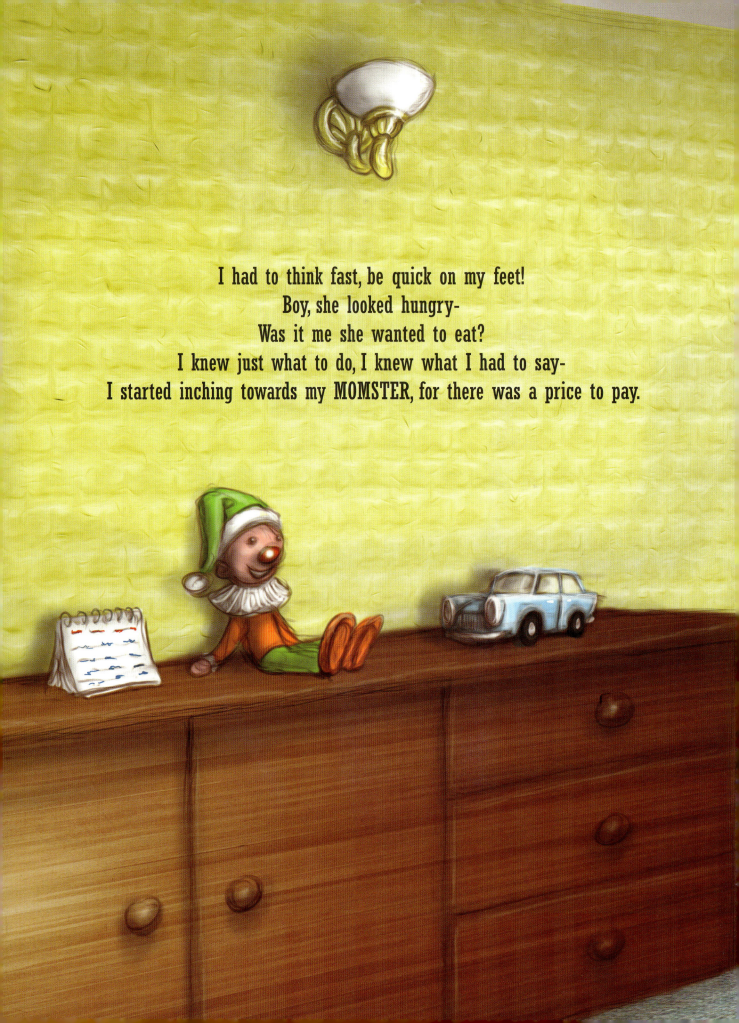

I had to think fast, be quick on my feet!
Boy, she looked hungry-
Was it me she wanted to eat?
I knew just what to do, I knew what I had to say-
I started inching towards my MOMSTER, for there was a price to pay.

I gently hugged my angry MOMSTER, cautious, she looked crazy-
I whispered in her pointy ear, "I'm sorry for being so lazy."
"I should've come when you asked, instead I chose to ignore-
Plus, I know that we've discussed this a million times before."

Her jaw unclenched, she straightened up -WHEW- my mom was back.

Respect your mom, kiss her often, and please treat her with care-
But NEVER forget, beneath that soft skin, a MOMSTER lives in there!

About the Author:

Laura Jensen-Kimball is the mother of four children and wife to Jeff. She was inspired to write after her youngest child was diagnosed with a speech delay. Books were a common tool used in improving his speech. Laura writes books with a touch of humor she feels both parent and child will enjoy. Living in Norwalk, Iowa, she is also a Registered Nurse currently pursuing her Masters in Nursing. This is Laura's first self-published book and hopes to publish her other stories soon- The Lonely Lap, Out of the Mouths of Moms, TREASUREJACK, Soldier in the Outfield, The Oak Tree Bully and Dear Mr. Wasn't Me. Check out Laura's website at **Wackystackbooks.com.**

About the Illustrator:

Peter Mahr is a children's book illustrator from Budapest, Hungary. He prefers handmade artwork styles by using pencil drawings with digital colorization and less digital effects. After leaving art school, Peter's work was mostly focused on China ink drawings and charcoal based images with additional acrylic coloring. Peter describes his style as "figurative expressionism." After becoming a father of two wonderful children, he focuses on illustrations for children. His son and daughter are his main inspirations. Find Peter at **Petermahr.wordpress.com**